Dedicated to Caroline who teaches us so much and loves so many.

The Integrity of the Journey

"A Smooth Stone"

First, I want to thank you for taking the time to read a little about our life's Journey. My Journey is forever and ever intertwined with my wife's, Carol. We were high school sweethearts and we remain sweethearts today after nearly 45 years of marriage. Together we have experienced many moves, many pets, many thrills, and many fabulous adventures, we even went to Japan one time! We have had a cat named Eddie Farmer, a black dog named Spot, but above all else we have two wonderful children, Chris, our son and Caroline. They have each now created the most wonderful and diverse families of their own. Chris married Kelly Marie Harris in 1994 – she has proven to be over and above the expectations or heights of what a couple envisions as a daughter-in-law and mother of their grandchildren. She is amazing to the core! They have our two grandchildren, Sarah Grace and Amelia. Caroline married Robert St. John on June 9, 2012 and he is proving to be more than we could have expected in a son-in-law. I call him often and ask him how things are in "Son-in- Law Land" – his sense of humor is a little tilted like mine – I love it!

Above all else in this little book I want to convey to you how my/our immense Trust in God has been built. It has not come easy. It has come on some very tough and arduous twists and turns. In the end I think I have come to understand that is what makes the Journey so much sweeter. The difficult times make the good times even more satisfying. I am a country boy at heart and I like to talk in stories. My mother's family all are great story tellers and I suppose I inherited that from the McCurdy side of my family. So it is now time for us to embark on this story about Love, Hope and Trust in God

Let me give you a brief background about how this all evolved. I am a native of Rockdale County Georgia, Milstead and Conyers, Ga. to be exact. I played Football at the University of

Georgia. I owned my own business in Conyers for 30 years. I was getting ready to retire in 2005 and I received a call from a dear friend, Edna Vaughan at The Upper Room in Nashville, Tennessee. Yep, that Upper Room, the one that publishes the little devotional magazine we are all so familiar with, "The Upper Room". She was making contact for Tom Albin, the Program Director at The Upper Room at that time. They were exploring the possibility of me taking charge and becoming the International Lay Director of Chrysalis, the world wide Youth program that works hand in hand with the Adult program, The Walk to Emmaus. I was baffled and intrigued by the notion. I had been involved as a volunteer in both programs for nearly 12 years at that point. Both The Walk to Emmaus and Chrysalis had played very prominent roles in my growth as a Christian. They are both very meaningful and worthwhile movements. As we talked and as I got deeper into this whole process my prayer changed from "God why should I do this to - God why should I **_NOT_** do this?" I became International Lay Director of Chrysalis in 2006 with a 3 year commitment.

When I assumed that role I jumped in enthusiastically head over heels. It was a life changing experience for me. I could literally see the lives of the people God had entrusted us with change. There was something about this movement that was almost tangible but I could not lay my hands or mind on it. Then one night it hit me - all of these "things" - these parts - are just parts in the makeup of a Journey that we are all on. We all have our own individual Journey that has been laid out for us. I came to understand that it does not matter how rich the Journey is, how poor it is, how happy it is, how sad it is or whatever. It was still our own individual Journey that was laid out for us before the foundation of the world was. I was satisfied with the overall premise of the Journey but it still did not tie in together with what I wanted our Leadership and our joint Journey together at Chrysalis to be like. Something was still missing.

Carol and I had been invited to a conference of College Ministries in Atlanta. It had nothing to do with the Chrysalis movement, yet it had all to do with the movement. Our friend Gregg Johnson was the leader, coordinator and sponsor of the event. I went to a break out session entitled "Leadership – Joshua Style". I was drawn in immediately because Joshua has been and will always be my Biblical hero. He was content to be second in command until God called him to be the Leader. I loved the break out session – I don't even remember the young man's name that led it. He was probably 30 years old - **maybe**? A young guy in his own right. The magic hit when he gave this analogy. He asked, "Can you imagine this conversation? OK Joshua – Moses is dead!! He is **DEAD**!! Now it is your time to be the Leader! Everything I have promised Moses I will give to you". Then the break out leader went on to explain that we all are on a Journey (I jumped up in my seat), he said it is just like the Disciples when Jesus was crucified. They did what Integrity told them to do – they went into the Upper Room and prayed. Wow!! You can't make this stuff up!! Right then and there I had the moniker for my term of Leadership of The International Chrysalis movement. Put Integrity into it. It does not matter how lonely etc. etc. What matters is the Integrity that you put into **THAT** Journey, **YOUR** Journey - that was it! That was the birth of my impetus - "The Integrity of the Journey". God continued to expound on this for me over the next few months and years. I came to believe that Integrity is what you do when no one else is watching. I was on a worldwide stage and I had lots of people watching – but what mattered most was not what I said but what I did. What did I do when they were **NOT** watching? That was the point.

I want to tell you that this little book has been hard. It has opened up some very hard memories and made me relive them. It has above all cemented my belief in God. My belief in His Grace and my belief in his Mercy. Carol and I have been down a very dark and lonely path on our Journey but now we are looking at sunshine! Today life is good! There is a saying where I come from that goes like this. "My future is so bright I gotta wear sunglasses!" I want you to read with us. Let us bare our souls to you and then ask you to join us in celebrating life and celebrating all the little things that God gives us and does for us – even when we don't expect it.

I get to share this news a lot now. I have grown from a cold hardnosed business man – an ex-UGA Football player on a very big stage to the most fulfilling thing I could have ever imagined. God has prepared me over all these years and all these business meetings and all these speaking engagements and all these experiences for my mission in life now. After this leg of our Journey with Caroline, Emory University Hospital asked me to be a PFA. I am a Patient Family Advisor on the Leukemia floor at Emory. I get to go around and chat with the patients and their caregivers. I tell them I am not going to stick them, poke them, or invade any part of their body. I am not a Doctor, I am not a Nurse, and I am not a Preacher but I can talk about a little bit of all those things. I tell them that what I am is a Dad that has a daughter that has survived Leukemia and is now thriving. I am simply there to offer them Love and Hope and Encouragement but above all else try to instill Trust into their hearts. My stage is now one on one with critically ill patients and those that love them the most, their families.

Let me invite you now to join me on my Journey.

Acts 1:8 "You will receive power when the Holy Spirit comes upon you, and you will be my witnesses in Jerusalem, Judea, Samaria and unto the ends of the Earth".

Chapter One

"The Philistine"

"And David with his sling in his hand reached down into the brook and took five smooth stones, he placed them in the pouch of his shepherd's bag, and with his sling in his hand he drew near to the Philistine". **1 Samuel 17: 40**

Fighting Giants – study – Max Lucado – Facing Your Giants – I have always taken pride in the fact I felt like that was my call – now I am **in the story** with David – I am getting older – I am not the young tight end anymore – my hair is gray – I DON'T WEIGH 235 anymore! I face a giant everyday – I draw back to Joshua and the promise God made to him – and the admonition God gave him – "Be strong and courageous" – that was the same courage he gave to David – just get 5 smooth stones and then Draw near to the Philistine (Reference to the scripture 1 Sam 17: 32-51)

These were the notes I wrote to myself on 10/26/08. I had done a study on the Max Lucado book "Facing Your Giants" – I thought my story would be very neat and concise – with real clean edges you know? I was supposed to start teaching it in two weeks to a group of young men. I knew if I was going to teach it, I would have to live it out in some way – my small thinking had pictured a flat tire on the way to the grocery store! So I was ready for the Bible Study – Yep a good story to tell about!

But now it is much different than I had envisioned. I stand next to a brook; it is 3:15 AM on Monday, September 6, 2010 – Labor Day. I sit next to the brook but the brook doesn't look anything like I expected, thought, or dreamed it would look like. It looks much different. I can barely stand to look at it or smell the stench that it is producing. This brook does not flow with clean clear water – refreshing to the touch – refreshing to the soul – refreshing to the lips or refreshing to the tongue. This brook is meandering with highly waxed shiny tile floors. They lead like a maze to who knows where. Its little tributaries are fed by elevators. They duck in and out of hallways – down long corridors with signs on them that say something like "Restricted Area – Do Not Enter". They say things like "Radiology" – they say things like "Surgical Area". The brook I am sitting by says "Hematology Unit" – it bears signs that warn against exposing the inhabitants of this brook area to foreign germs and infections. This brook flows through the heart of Emory University Hospital – Sixth Floor – East Wing.

Two days earlier it was to be a glorious day in the South - Saturday morning, September 4th. I went outside my house and felt just a hint of coolness in the air. A neighbor couple, the McRobbies, walked by with their twin Cairn Terriers tugging at their leashes, biting and straining against them to hurry up and let's get home! I yell at them, "It's Game Day in the South"!! I was loading up to go see my beloved Georgia Bulldogs open another Football season. I was taking my son Chris and his family, my daughter-in-law Kelly and my beautiful granddaughter, Sarah Grace. Georgia is set to kick off in an early game – kick off at 12:20. Chris and Kelly celebrated their 16th wedding anniversary yesterday. My family gathered at our house for supper. My daughter Caroline and her boyfriend Robert had joined us. We had a great time, just sitting around the dinner table loving on each other; them aggravating me and me playing along with it. It was great but Caroline was not feeling well. She tried her best to join in the nonsense but she just didn't have the gas to run on. She looked tired and her color was terrible. She hardly ate. Little did I know that there was a Giant lurking around my house. He was sizing it up. He was ready to take what he thought was his. I didn't realize that he was beginning to roar at the top of his lungs, but I knew in my heart that something wasn't right. Caroline had been sick for about 3 weeks. She had been to the Doctor with her flu like symptoms. They were treating her for bronchitis but she was not responding, in fact she seemed to be getting worse. The water in the brook was now getting very murky.

On Friday night as we were chatting, Mom (Carol) brought up the subject that if Caroline did not feel better soon we need to consider taking her to Emory for a look. I didn't really think much about it other than to reminisce about our stays at Emory. Me with neck surgery, my mother in law, my mother and various other stays over the past 35 years. It was a safe place, an intimidating place, but a place that we had absolute confidence in if we got sick. Well to make a long story short as we traveled to Athens my wife Carol had spent a terrible and long night with Caroline. She could not get any rest – Carol made the "Mom Call" – she loaded Caroline up and headed to Atlanta and Emory. They sent us a text message and said they were heading over there. I was not overly concerned – I just thought "OK, she will get a different look now". In my head we would all go on our merry way after the game and meet back up in Greensboro that night. The Giant was growing!

We packed up and headed out for the short drive to Athens and the game. It was a beautiful day. We park with the Georgia Football Lettermen in our lot across from Sanford Stadium. Sarah Grace had made a new friend; we had been visiting with Jimmy Wood, one of my old team mates from the 60's. Now our grandkids were playing with each other. Wow, it couldn't get much better than this. We went to the game and Georgia thoroughly trounced their opponent. As the 4th quarter of the game began, I got a call from Carol. She said she thought I needed to head over to Emory that Caroline was sick – to be exact she said she was real sick. We began getting our things together to leave. A few minutes later Carol called back. I sensed the desperation beginning to grow in her voice. She wanted to know if I could get in touch with Robert, Caroline's boyfriend who was at the game with another group of friends. The Giant had pulled his sword and was swinging it now with all his might! We headed out toward Emory and another call – this time she said that it did not look good – to hurry but be careful. I was sick – deep in my heart – deep in my gut I was sick! This was my baby – this was my 34 year old baby. This was my baby that I would protect with my life.

This was my baby that was the joy of my life. This was my baby that had gone to South Central Los Angeles to minister in that urban environment right out of college. This was my baby that was now a teacher at Heritage High School in Conyers, Ga. She works with the 9th grade Academy there. This was my baby! Carol did not verbalize what the problem was; she just said it did not look good. Then the bombshell – the first lob from the Giant; all she said was they checked her blood and her white cell count was 70,000 and the red cell count was dismally low. My heart sank. I know enough about medicine to know that a high white cell count is not good. A word flashed through my mind but I would not say it. I would not verbalize it; I would not give it life. The Giant had it in his hand –he was standing there tossing it up and down in the air with his big old right hand. Just nonchalantly tossing that word up and down real slow like and grinning. I could not bear to think it.

Carol called again as I got on North Decatur Road leading to Emory. This time she was near to tears. I knew the desperation in the voice of my wife of 41 years. She asked where I was and had I gotten in touch with Robert? She wanted to make sure Chris and Kelly were with me. I told her we were about 10 minutes away and that's when she said, "Caroline wanted me to tell you that we are on the 6th floor in the East Wing; that is the hematology ward and she did not want you to be scared when you got here."

The Giant had just tossed the word high in the air and impaled it with his spear! I told Carol in that instant "I have a word floating in my head that I cannot say" She asked "What is that word?" I said "Leukemia" and she began to cry. She said "Yes.... that is the word". My world came crashing at my feet with that word. Leukemia. **Nothing** – I reiterate **Nothing** - could have been further from my mind. Just to describe the shock is not possible. My hands had gone numb on the steering wheel. Chris and Kelly were in the car right in front of me; Carol had already prepared them so they could deal with me. We both pulled into the valet parking at the same time. Chris and I got out of our cars at the same time and both began to cry. Not Caroline, this could not be! I could only pray that tomorrow, **oh tomorrow**, would get better!

"My Prayers Go Deeper"

Chapter Two

The First Night

Jehovah-Jireh

"Do not lay a hand on the boy," he said. "Do not do anything to him. Now I know that you fear God, because you have not withheld from me your son, your only son. Abraham looked up and there in a thicket he saw a ram caught by its horns. He went over and took the ram and sacrificed it as a burnt offering instead of his son. So Abraham called that place The LORD *Will Provide. And to this day it is said, "On the mountain of the* LORD *it will be provided."* **Gen. 22:12-14**

We were in shock. How could this be? I'm at a Georgia Football game and Carol calls me to come home – "Caroline is real sick and being admitted to Emory; by the way they are putting her on the hematology floor". No mention up front of Leukemia. Carol spared me that news until I arrived at Emory. She knew I would be in a mess after she told me. She was right! I went to Valet parking and got the car situated and met up with Chris and Kelly. Chris and I fell into each other's arms right there in Valet parking. Weeping for a daughter; weeping for a sister. I gathered the strength and we found Emory University Hospital, Floor 6E Room 614. Those are names and numbers that are indelibly etched into my soul forever. Sort of like remembering dates that things happened. Those are the numbers I associate with Caroline's diagnosis. When I got to the room I basically fell across Caroline's bed, I couldn't help from crying. There lay my baby – incredibly sick, helpless and scared to death. In the last few hours she and her Mama had been told "You have Leukemia – you have Acute Leukemia – she may not have lasted 7 more days – rejoice that you got her on up here to us"! All of this had been met with amazing denial on our part. "NO you cannot be correct in this!! What is "ACUTE"? What did I do to cause this? Could we have prevented this? What will happen to her?" All of these answers were to come rapidly I would soon find out, but first things first.

By the time I got there the staff had already begun the blood transfusions. I won't get into the mechanics of Acute Leukemia but basically your blood begins to become non-functioning. The body is producing immature white blood cells that basically do nothing but crowd out the good cells. The red count goes drastically down because they can't mature, the white count goes drastically up because they know there is an invasion of some type, the immature white cells multiply at an exponential rate and the body cannot regenerate itself. A tragic downhill slide begins if nothing is done. The immediate help is new blood – transfusions. I don't know how many they gave her, but it was a lot.

I had been murmuring to myself all the way up to the floor and into her room, "Lord help her! Lord help her! Lord help her!" My mind was racing such that I could not stop long enough to verbalize a real prayer. I basically did not know what to pray other than to ask God to help her. I was assimilating as much information as I could in those first few minutes. I couldn't think straight – Leukemia?? Where did this come from?? They told me that Acute Leukemia means rapid onset and that it needed a rapid response because it acted so quickly. They knew upfront it was Acute Leukemia but they did not know what strain of Acute Leukemia it was. That would come after a bone marrow biopsy. That was not a very pleasant thought either! Everything they told me I could only think to utter, "Lord help her"! I don't know how deep those prayers were going but I do think that they were honored by God and that they actually got past the ceiling of the room we were in, Emory University Hospital, floor 6E, Room 614 – remember that! That would become our sanctuary over the next few months. That would be our Cathedral, our Holy Place, and our place of Rest. This would be our command center.

I know there is no place "scores" are kept as to prayers and how effective they are. I do know that over the next month we would not lift our head up in Room 614 without saying a prayer. My prayer was constant. "Lord, help her" Then I added "and have Mercy on her". Caroline had been the model daughter every mother and father dream of. Excellent daughter, exemplary student, great friend, mentor, example, little sister, wonderful Aunt, Missionary, and Teacher – you name it and her name was at the top of the list.

Now she lay here helpless and worn out from this stupid disease. We kept asking why? I kept wondering how deep my prayers were going. I know that in those days of anguish in room 614 that God took me deeper. He took me to places that only He inhabits and will occasionally let someone have a glimpse of – if they only ask. I did ask - I changed my prayers from "Please" to "Lord I am grateful that I get to see your mighty hand at work!" Only God could have begun the slow and wonderful process of recovery that we witnessed.

The staff at Emory could not have been any better. The nurses with their compassion and caring; the Doctors with their dignity and an assuring sense of purpose in every step they made and every course of action they described. The Pharmacists, the Technicians, Housekeeping, Food Service, everyone!

I knew that my prayers were going deeper and deeper because God kept sending those people that we needed in our lives at exactly that moment to walk with us hand-in-hand down this lonely and confusing road we now found ourselves on. Me trusting God with my daughter's life, Him providing what I was asking for through the hands and feet of the staff at Emory University Hospital. The amazing thing that I would come to understand was that God was also trusting ME! He would not put on us more that we could endure at that moment, but then when we were at our lowest point He would reaffirm that He could be trusted. It actually began at lunch on the next day, the first full day at Emory. The initial day had been a long and shocking day - beginning in the most benign way – us doing our ordinary thing and attending a UGA football game in Athens, then the summons to get over to Emory, then the shocking news of Leukemia! We spent the rest of that first night making arrangements – calling friends, calling loved ones, getting things set up for the long haul there at Emory. Sleeping on the floor and sleeping in a chair.

After that fitful first night, at Lunch the next day Carol and I went down to get a meal in the cafeteria at the Hospital. My son Chris and Caroline's boyfriend Robert would remain in 614 with her. We got our trays of food and sat down at the table. We looked at each other and immediately burst into tears. We had tried to maintain our composure in the room with Caroline because we did not want her to see us losing control of ourselves. Now we were sobbing our hearts out. I felt a hand on my shoulder and a beautiful young lady, a total stranger, had her hands on mine and Carol's shoulders. She began to pray the most soothing and compassionate prayer I had ever heard. She asked God to comfort us in our time of need. It was the most comforting and reassuring prayer I have ever heard or experienced. When she finished praying I stood up, we thanked her for her prayers and we all hugged. She went on her unassuming way and we never saw her again. God had sent an angel to reassure us that now He was in control.

So then I knew it to be true. He would send a good report, or a new protocol, a new Health Specialist, or a new friend! He would send what we needed. He reaffirmed over and over that He can be trusted. He provided over and over significant visual proof to me that He was trustworthy. But you know what slowly but surely became so apparent to me? It was the fact that God trusted **_ME_**!! He trusted me to tell this story. He did not want Caroline's suffering to go in vain – He wanted me to tell the story of His amazing grace, of His compassion and sensitivity. He wanted to show to the world and especially to me that **_YES_** indeed my prayers were going deeper. He was hearing them specifically and He was responding. I had a job

- 15 -

to do. That job was to let go of my control and approach this whole matter with child life faith. I know how cheesy that sounds but after I have realized **what** God did - **how** He did it -and now beginning to understand **why** He did it. I know without a doubt in my mind that my prayers did go deeper. They went to the soul of my being but they went to the heart of Jesus. We asked; he delivered. Now I **HAVE** to tell you what I often tell my friends – "If you are looking for God to show up in a jet plane, He will show up in a row boat every time!!" Meaning by this that we are so specific and finite in our prayers most of the time that we only expect God to respond in a certain way. The reason for that is that we are so limited within our own boundaries and expectations. We are limited by **OUR** world and our world view and our perspectives and our expectations. God is not. He will often provide in the most unexpected of ways. He will use the most ordinary to do the most extra ordinary. I was about to see this first hand and to see how real God was.

Chapter Three

Joy comes in the morning

"Weeping may last for the night – but Joy comes in the morning" **Psalms 30:5**

"Tomorrow" did come and we began our Journey. The shock of yesterday had been almost unbearable. The only thing we knew was that Caroline had been diagnosed with a broad diagnosis of Leukemia. The only thing Carol and our family knew was that according to the movies that was supposed to be a virtual death sentence. I had no idea of the Hope that was also available with this diagnosis. The staff had given us pamphlets to read and many websites etc. I have to tell you that only served to scare me to death. We had not even met her primary staff of attendants yet. Carol had slept on the floor and I had slept in that hospital extension chair in the room. Wow!! Neither of us had basically slept at all that first night. Robert, Caroline's boyfriend and my son Chris and his family, Kelly and Sarah Grace had been there too. We were all scared to death. We were paralyzed with apprehension. We had immense trust in God but we had never been called on to go to the very roots of that Trust. We had never been called on to trust God for the very life of our daughter. We were now in that position. We were to place our daughter into the skilled hands of the medical staff at Emory University Hospital. We had no idea what the face of compassion would look like. We were to quickly find out.

Bright and early on that first full day, two of the cutest, loveliest, most energetic, spunkiest people you have ever laid eyes on bounced into the room. They said, "Hi I'm Amy and I'm Joy. We are going to take care of you today!" See my daughter was 34 years old at the time and is a 9th grade teacher at Heritage High School in Conyers, Ga. God totally knew who and what it would take to get Caroline settled down and it was these two! First thing they did was get Caroline relaxed, answered questions, prepped her for her upcoming procedures and smiled an awful lot!! Lordy – they got to talking to Caroline and you would have thought the Sorority meeting had broken out in Caroline's room! They encouraged us to make her room comfy so we immediately began the process of planning how to turn her room into her home away from home. We began to plan the move of her favorite items from her home in Conyers into Room 614 on Floor 6E – the Leukemia ward. With the help of the girls we would make it just like home. They were relentless in their care and compassion for Caroline.

Next came the real big guns!! Dr. Morgan McLemore, Dr. Hue, Dr. Ping, Marian. Dr. McLemore and his staff were there to describe what the immediate procedures and the game plan would be. They may as well been speaking an ancient foreign language to me! They were talking about bone marrow biopsies, lumbar punctures, drawing blood, infusing blood, chemotherapy, PICC lines, how to eat, how not to eat, and above all **GERMS**!! Sterilization, cleanliness, a virtual quarantine from the outside world. **NO LIVE FLOWERS!!** All of this designed not to intimidate or alarm us but to educate us on the best way possible to follow a protocol to insure Caroline's recovery. We asked a million questions, Caroline joined in the questioning but she basically allowed us to do the talking. She wanted to know what was going to happen to her but she knew that we were so worked up that there would be very few subjects that we could skip over. She was right. We asked the minutest questions down to "should we remove our shoes in the room??" When that flurry of attention was over, several things still remained. First was our concern, second was our task of converting her room, third was the Leukemia, next was Caroline's request that we not leave her alone, and lastly was Amy and Joy! How I thank God for the last two. They were exactly what Caroline needed at that moment in her life.

Caroline then began the process of being compliant and moving forward, no; almost attacking her treatment, with a fierceness that I knew was inside of her. She began giving instructions on what to bring from home and where to put it in the room. Amy and Joy would cheer and say "Yeah!!.... bring it!!" They would encourage Caroline and tell her how cute that was going to be! Three little girls playing house!

The main thing Caroline told us she wanted was her art and music - her iTunes and a speaker system. She didn't want to be alone. Her art and her music would be constant companions – bringing some normalcy in her now new life. Amy and Joy would help usher that new life in with compassion and skill. Amy was the seasoned nurse on 6E – she knew her "stuff" inside and out. Joy was the new kid on the block. She had 14 years experience at Children's Health Care of Atlanta, working with pediatric Leukemia patients. She had never worked with adults before, this was her first day on the job at Emory working with adults and Caroline was her first patient. She later confessed to us that she had cried all the way to work that morning driving in from LaGrange, Ga. because she was so scared. God knew what was best for all concerned. That it would take someone with experience and the skill to handle children to handle our fragile Caroline. It would take someone with the compassion and caring of Caroline to encourage and strengthen Joy. Carol told Joy on that first morning, "The greatest thing you can ever do for anyone is what you do for their child". Joy soon realized that everyone on that floor- all those adults were someone's child.

Chapter Four

"Transformation – Part One"

<u>Art – The Mind and Spirit</u>

"Consider the Sparrow"

"Are not two sparrows sold for a penny? Yet not one of them will fall to the ground outside your Father's care. And even the very hairs of your head are all numbered. So don't be afraid; you are worth more than many sparrows." **Matthew 10:29-31**

Ok - the planning was over. I can truly and literally say that Joy came in the morning of that first day. It had been good for Joy and it had also been good for Caroline

Now it was time for action. Caroline, Amy and Joy had given us our marching orders for the day. Let me interject here that Caroline is very task oriented. One of the first things she told Joy and Amy was to write on the dry erase board in her room their goals for that day. Whether it be as mundane as take a bath or as arduous as a bone marrow biopsy – she wanted it on the board and she wanted it checked off when it was behind her. No more looking backwards, only looking forward to the next task at hand. They all three had given Robert and Chris specific orders on what to go fetch from home. Luckily she only lives about 30 minutes from Emory so it is not an overwhelming task to head out to Conyers for something – especially something that will make her life better right now. This period of her life was obviously going to be spent in the confines of 614 so we all wanted to make it as natural and comfortable for her as possible. Mind you, Carol and I were still sleeping in chairs those first nights – we had not gotten into our routine yet.

The boys took off – Robert to Conyers and Chris to Greensboro with a list of things to bring from home. The obvious was clothing and personal items. Past that the list got pretty short due to the nature of her illness and the nature of her isolation. No need for books. A friend from childhood Meg, would take care of that little matter. Unbeknownst to Meg about the germs – quarantine – isolation etc., the worst thing Caroline could have or do was to place her hands all over books that had been in a Library or even worse on a shelf in a public place exposed to all types sneezes, coughs, snot, spit, well you get the picture! Meg in her thoughtfulness sent her a Kindle – an electronic book. Any subject matter at your finger tips – simple -select and download!! No hassle – it was clean out of the box – no germs – voila!! Caroline's insatiable appetite for Literature could be handled in a very efficient way – thank you God for spurring Meg on to send such a thoughtful gift at such an appropriate time!

Caroline had a TV in the room (although it was hardly ever turned on). No need for flowers since she could not be around the germs and creepy crawlies in the dirt. No need for make up since she could not wear any. It boiled down to sort of like "OK you are going to be stranded on a desert island for 5 months – what do you want to take with you?" Decisions, decisions, decisions!

Well here you go on her list of "**must haves**". First and foremost were her paintings. Caroline is a tremendous Artist. That is her release and the way she expresses herself – in oils on a canvas. I have a virtual gallery of her work in my house. She does bold vivid colors and the thing I like most about it is that she remains true to the "little girl" still trapped inside her adult body. She has never stayed inside the lines!! That is what makes her work so intriguing to me. She can just start and it flies from the brush into the most poignant imaginative work you can ever visualize. Autumn leaves floating on a pond. An abstract of the view off our porch in the Mountains of North Georgia - the Chattahoochee National Forest. A tree limb that encompasses 3 different canvasses and three different sections of the limb. It is simply amazing. A lot of them are things she has done or seen and then how it goes onto oil and a canvas through the filter of her imagination.

There is one in particular that she loves; a picture of an empty bird cage. Caroline had explained she got the idea from an Emily Dickinson poem – "Hope is the thing with feathers". Staying true to herself Caroline paraphrased it to say "Hope is a thing with Feathers". A trivial sub of "A" for"THE" but that makes the story even more relative to our lives. Remember the little girl that can't stay inside the lines?? That picture had been hanging in her Living Room for several years.

What was the significance of an empty cage? What does that represent? I don't know where the model for the cage came from but it is beautiful. The striking thing about it is that the cage is empty – it is sitting there in its elegance – empty. Not holding anything, not trapping anything – just the cage; a symbol of many different things to many different folks. It just depends on how you look at it!

Where did Hope play into the painting? Where did it come from? What is the "Hope"? Hope for freedom? Hope for a companion? Hope for food? Hope for water? Hope for the cage to spring open? Hope for what? I have come to believe it is Hope for something that I cannot see – but something that I know is real and that I know will come. Hope for the love of God and the Mercy that He will show us. The poem goes like this:

"Hope is the thing with feathers"

"Hope" is the thing with feathers that perches in the soul, and sings the tune without the words, and never stops at all,

And sweetest in the Gale is heard, and sore must be the storm that could abash the little bird that kept so many warm,

I've heard it in the chilliest land, and on the strangest Sea, yet never in Extremity had it asked a crumb of me.

Emily Dickinson © 1861

When we had gazed at that painting on the wall in Caroline's Living Room in Conyers we never knew that God would be preparing us for the day we would hear the word Leukemia, but He was.

Without rehashing the story again Carol had taken Caroline to Emory University Hospital to find out why she could not shake this "Flu" we all thought she had. The rest of our family and I had taken off for the Georgia Football game in Athens. Not having any idea how the course of our lives was about to change so drastically with the sound of one word, one sentence. "I'm sorry but I have some shocking news for you, you have Leukemia!" Carol was knocked off her feet and Caroline could not bear to hear what she had just heard. The word Leukemia had ushered in to their minds all the graphic images from the TV and from the Movies. Chemo and funerals and weeping parents and loved ones and lost hope and all the drama that goes with that word, Leukemia.

That was a Saturday and we had to wait on the minutes to slowly tick by that first weekend to find out exactly what type of Leukemia she had and all the prep work that goes with the treatment regimen. Bone marrow biopsy first, then the wait for the blood analysis to tell the tale of exactly how to proceed. Then surgery for the insertion of the PICC line - that's the port system that all the blood work inflow and outflow goes through. I think it is inserted into the Jugular vein. Our family had rallied in room 614 at Emory. We were beside ourselves but we held this deep assurance that God was with us the whole time. We would look at each other and begin to cry. And then there was Robert! Caroline's boyfriend at the time. I knew he was special but I was soon to find out exactly how special he was. See Robert is a lot like me – he thinks outside the box – he sort of marches to the beat of another drummer. He got there late on Saturday night from the UGA game as well. He immediately began to reassure Caroline and all of us that things would be all right. He was the voice of optimism during all this. After being given his assignment by the girls, he went home on Sunday afternoon to make his arrangements at work and all. He moved her precious things from home into her new temporary home – Room 614 Emory University Hospital 6E. The main thing he brought was that picture of the bird cage. He hung it directly on the wall in front of her bed. That is what she looked at all day long. When he marched into the room with all that "stuff" he pronounced to Caroline. "Well I'm like Cortez – I burned my ships!!" She said what do you mean? He answered, "Well Cortez burned his ships so he could not go home – I quit my job today and I am going to stay right here with you until you get well"! That was the beginning of stuff that you can't make up!!

Monday came and the barrage of Doctors with final analysis and reports of all the tests. Acute Lymphoblastic Leukemia – a real big scary title. Then came all the support telling Caroline and us what to expect next. Doctors, Nurses, Pharmacists, Dieticians, Chaplains, Technicians, House Keeping, they were all great. Then a final visit from the Administrative Staff – they had to make sure the Insurance was in place, the Health Care Directives, the Power of Attorney and all those things. He needed to talk about the Insurance. Caroline is a Teacher at Heritage High School in Conyers, Ga. I came to realize how great their insurance is. The man looked at Caroline and said the costs of this treatment will be huge. He specifically used the word "Catastrophic", Carol was trying to lessen the impact and she blurted out to him in front of Caroline, "You don't have to talk about that now!" He was loving, patient, kind, and reassuring and with all the Grace in the world he simply looked at Carol and said, "Yes we do - She needs to understand what is about to happen". They discussed it all in depth and he left – the word "Catastrophic" hanging in Carol's mind. She looked at Caroline and they looked at each other – then the magic hit. Caroline looked at the picture she had painted once upon a time in her leisure and now it spoke to the depths of all our souls. She looked at the picture of the empty bird cage and the line *"Hope is a thing with feathers"* and with all the conviction in the world asked her mother. "Mom, what about the Sparrow?" She knew God would take care of her and supply all her needs.

The God of Hope

"May the God of hope fill you with all joy and peace as you trust in him, so that you may overflow with hope by the power of the Holy Spirit." **Romans 15:13**

A bird – an empty cage – a daughter scared to death – a family willing to do anything to make her better – a loving caring boyfriend who would burn his ships and remain by her side through the worst of times and then become her husband – a niece who so desperately wanted a little brother or sister – a brother and sister-in-law that had tried to fulfill that wish of their 8 year old daughter but could not – that brother that had told his little girl that God decides when life starts and when life ends and we just had to wait for His plan – then in the darkest of hours when we thought there was no Hope God grants the simple prayer of an 8 year old girl and sends a baby sister, Amelia Caroline Ingle to fulfill her big sister's dreams. A high school football team that would paint their shoes orange in honor of Caroline - the famous University of Georgia Head Football Coach Vince Dooley who would call this old player of his and tell him that in the end there is **ALWAYS** Hope! A loyal friend named Loran Smith, who is a Leukemia survivor himself, that would call and proclaim that there is **ALWAYS** Hope! Most especially, an old teammate of this dad, Dr. Tommy Lawhorne, he called or made contact every day to check on things. Every day he either called or sent a text to see how we were doing - how was I doing? Every day! He took the time.

Who would have known when we as a group heard that word, Leukemia, on September 4th, 2010 that we as a family would fall on our face and worship Him as the God of Hope?

Chapter Five

The Transformation - the Music

"Body and Soul"

"You will seek me and find me, when you seek me with your whole heart" **Jer. 29:13**

Lord my prayer today is that I can let go of those things that do not draw me closer to you and that you show me what to throw out in my life as I seek you with my whole heart –

LWI from Room 614

"Add to the Beauty" Sara Groves

Now it was time for more action. Caroline, Amy and Joy had taken care of the visual part of the transformation. Now it was time for Robert and Chris to kick in as only a brother and boyfriend can. Now came the music! Caroline so desperately wanted to remain somewhat normal. Her music would be part of that anchor to her regular life. Our whole family has always been wrapped up in music. It has been the barometer of our souls, the gauge by which our temperament could be measured. Happy – get a happy song, sad – pull out a tear jerker, need inspiration – tap into the music. Music has always played a tremendous role in my personal life. I like all of it but I like it stabbing me in the heart. Whether it is a tragic Country song (who can't love "and she got ran over by that old train")? Or an over the top love song –Unchained Melody by the Righteous Brothers -"Oh my love, my darling I hunger for your touch" or a soul soothing rendition of the Psalms by John Michael Talbot – Psalms 62 – "Only in God is my salvation". It has always moved me.

I guess one of my first real memories of how the music could affect me was when I was in my teens and I went to Ponce de Leon Park in Atlanta where the old Atlanta Crackers used to play baseball. I saw a young boy sing "Fingertips" and he was like 12 or 13 years old. His name was Little Stevie Wonder. I saw James Brown live singing "I feel good". I saw Elvis in concert. I have seen Willie Nelson numerous times. I still need to apologize to that guy at the Omni in Atlanta from long ago. We were there seeing Willie and I was standing up the whole show I was so excited. This guy behind me told me to sit down and I quickly responded to him, "I bought this seat from the floor all the way up to Heaven and I intend to use all that space tonight my friend – so get over it!" I was in my 30's. I need to track him down and apologize! Now I am in my 60's and my friend Bob See and I went to see a Kid Rock concert. I know that now I am getting paid back in spades for that quick retort I made to that man at the Willie concert. When Bob and I went to see Kid Rock a few years ago this guy stood up in front of us the whole night. I didn't say a word – I was not the least bit concerned that on that night he owned his seat from the floor all the way up to Heaven. Touché!!!!

<u>Caroline's music</u>: The boys took off for home with a list of things to bring back. She had her iPhone with her. It contained all of her music but she had no way of playing it in room 614. Chris, being the ever diligent brother that he is (I trained him well!!) had to take off to his home in Greensboro, Ga. to take care of his personal situations and make arrangements for his business to carry on . He told the office that he was available but would be on an extended absence hanging in with Caroline in room 614. He took care of his business and grabbed up his iHome or whatever his iPhone receiving dock is that is capable of playing music through it. You know it is one of those self contained little boxes that will charge the phone and allow you to play music through it as well. He threw that in the backpack with him to bring to Caroline. Little did we know that piece of equipment would change my life forever and possibly that of my whole family. Grace does come in the strangest of places!!

We had been passing the day away like this. Me sitting on one side of Caroline holding one hand, Robert sitting on the other side holding the other hand and Mom (Carol) doing what she does best and always instinctively on hospital stays or when one of her brood is very sick. She grabs the lotion and massages their feet – hoping to bring some comfort to her loved one while they are lying in that hospital bed. Believe me Caroline needed comfort in all kinds of ways in those days. Chris was always there and always the first one to run an errand. Need food – he's your man. Need toiletries – he's your man. Need something to read – he's your man. Need to just be loved by a big brother – he's your man.

Well Chris arrives back from Greensboro with his supplies in hand. He unloads stuff and then pulls out the music player. He ceremoniously plugs it into the wall and sits it in the window sill of 614. Caroline immediately requested one song – keep in mind she has thousands of songs on her iPhone. She requested "Add to the Beauty" by Sara Groves. We played it through and we all listened – I will confess to you now I had never heard that song before and for that matter I can't say that I was very familiar with Sara Groves. But she would change my life forever. For several years now when I teach Men's' Bible Studies I always encourage them in this way. You can change the world by changing yourself. You change yourself by transforming your mind. You seek God with your whole heart when you look for Him in all you say, all you do, and all you think. It is so effortless that as you go deeper and deeper it becomes so natural you don't even try. There is a bible verse that goes like this – Romans 12:1-2 "Therefore, I urge you brothers, in view of God's mercy, to offer your bodies as living sacrifices to God - this is your spiritual act of worship. Do not conform any longer to the pattern of this world, but be transformed by the renewing of your mind. Then you will be able to test and approve what God's will is – his good, pleasing and perfect will." Sara Groves was about to continue that radical transformation of my mind that had begun back in 1990.

In 1972 Carol and I had moved with my work to Birmingham, Ala. We had a newly born son, Chris. We had moved for me to be Assistant Terminal Manager at Roadway Express. The work was hard, the conditions were hard and life just in general was tough. I found myself reaching out for a spiritual anchor and did not have one. I met with Rev. Frank Barker the Pastor at Briarwood Presbyterian Church in Birmingham and gave my life to Christ in 1972. That was pretty simple – kneel down, pray a sincere prayer of forgiveness and ask Jesus to take control of my life. I did that and sincerely believed in all that I had just done and what it stood for. But I found myself later drifting back into old habits that I had formed. I won't get into detail but I sincerely believed that Jesus was my Savior but I realized He was not Lord of my life. Pride had me still hang on to certain things I would not relinquish. I found myself reaching another low spiritual point in my life and I needed more. I had to find out the root of my loneliness. I got my answer through my children again. Chris was at North Carolina State on a Football scholarship and his life had made a drastic u-turn. He had been injured and his hopes of a successful football career there was now over. Caroline had invited us to go to a new church that had just started up in Conyers. There were like 20 people there – most of them were kids Caroline's age, some with their parents some not. We met in the office of a company that sold masonry goods and equipment – rocks! Not very elegant or spiritual, but real world at its rawest and at its core. No pride displayed there at all. That was the exact kind of environment that God needed to get me in to go to my heart. There came a pivotal point in a morning service and the fathers were asked to pray for and bless their children. Well Chris was obviously not there and Caroline (who was 15 at the time) looked at me and I realized she had never heard me pray a real prayer, a sincere prayer from the heart for her or anyone else for that matter. I always deferred to their Mom, Carol for spiritual kinds of things. I looked real good but I was living a sham spiritually. I looked into Caroline's eyes and that is when the curtain tore for me – I saw Jesus clearly in her eyes in that old dilapidated rock quarry office. That began the transformation in my life.

I started listening to Christian music, not because I felt I had to but because I was just naturally drawn to it. A new kind of Christian music - not "everybody in their Choir Robe" hymns but real Christian music – sung by everyday people, doing everyday stuff. Worshipping in a different style than I had ever been accustomed to. I even went to a concert one night at a Church in Decatur, Ga. There was a Monk there singing that night named John Michael Talbot. I was changed forever. I knew that David had sung the Psalms but I had never heard anyone actually sing scripture. He sang a song that changed my life forever. The title of the song is "You will receive power". It is based on Acts 1:8."And you will receive power when the Holy Spirit comes upon you, and you will be my witnesses in Jerusalem, Judea, Samaria and unto the ends of the Earth." I had to live life and do some "experiencing" before I got to understand what I think "Power" means. I came to have an understanding that it meant that I would have the power to love, the power to give, the power to trust, the power to pray and the power to weep. It goes on to talk about Jerusalem, Judea and Samaria and the ends of the Earth. I came to understand the "Ends of the Earth" meant around my dinner table, it meant at the gas pump asking a stranger to pray for my daughter Caroline who had been diagnosed with Leukemia. It meant in room 614 at Emory. It meant being a Witness in everything I did and said. It meant being a witness at home and in Jerusalem. Let me explain.

One morning Carol and I needed a little break so we walked down to Emory Village to have lunch at one of the local restaurants right off campus at Emory. As we were returning and taking a stroll I spotted a man walking a couple of hundred yards in front of us. I noticed he had a yamakah (Jewish cap) on his head. I told Carol to go catch that guy I wanted to know if he was a rabbi. Some of my dearest friends are Jewish and I know how fervently they pray. I wanted the "Home Team" praying for my daughter. Carol succeeded in catching him and as I approached I asked "Sir, are you a rabbi?" He responded "No but I am Jewish". I then asked him if he would be so kind as to add my daughter's name to their prayer box so that his Synagogue could pray for her each morning. He took Caroline's name and assured me he would do such. I asked him what his name was and what he did at Emory. He told me his name, Dr. Michael Graiser, and that he worked in the lab that looked for matches for the bone marrow transplants to Leukemia patients. I explained that my daughter had just been diagnosed with Leukemia – you can't make this stuff up!! I did not hear from Dr. Graiser for several months, then one morning around Thanksgiving 2010 I got an email from Dr. Graiser. He assured me that he had followed through and his Synagogue had been praying for Caroline. He went on to tell me that he and his wife had been visiting their daughter in – you guessed it – Jerusalem!! He said they even left a prayer note for her in the Western Wall at Jerusalem!! Unbelievable! God was truly continuing to reveal his Mercy to us in a real and tangible way.

Sara Groves would now pick up the torch and usher us closer and closer to God.

As I said earlier I had never heard or consciously paid attention to Sara Groves as an artist. Caroline specifically requested that she be played and specifically play this one song entitled "Add to the Beauty". I had no idea what it was. It played and we were holding Caroline's hands and it was the most soothing thing to me. I tried to pay close attention to the words but I had to listen to it again. I had heard the words, but they had not moved to my heart I don't think. I asked Caroline what the artist was saying and then the magic hit. Caroline said, "She is saying I want to add to the beauty, I want to tell a better story". Tell a better story! Wow! Then Caroline said these words, "Dad I just want to live to tell a better story". That is when I went deeper. I too wanted to tell a better story. I wanted to tell one of success and not failure. I wanted to tell one of God's Mercy and His Grace. Not one of sorrow and suffering. I wanted to tell how God had healed my daughter, but it would take a long and arduous road to get to that point. All I could pray for was that day by day, minute by minute that we could indeed tell a better story than what we had just left. I got the words to the song and studied them. It told the entire story of our experience at Emory University Hospital. Here are the words to the song – I will try to explain how they played out in our lives day by day:

"Add to the Beauty"

Sara Groves

We come with beautiful secrets
We come with purpose written on our hearts, written on our souls
We come to every new morning
With possibilities only we can hold, that only we can hold

We come before God with requests and petitions that only we know. Some of those closest to us may know what we desire or ask for but for the most part they are known only to us, in the deepest part of our Soul. We are learning to live day by day and minute by minute as I said before. Each day brings a new dawn, a new possibility, a new revelation that only we see and only we experience.

Redemption comes in strange places, small spaces
Calling out the best of who we are

Oh how this resounds within us. God meets us in the strangest of places! It is usually not where we expect to meet Him; it is usually in the simplest circumstance in the most ordinary of places. A hospital room! It is there that we search the deepest and go the farthest to pray for the ones we love.

And I want to add to the beauty
To tell a better story

I want to shine with the light
That's burning up inside

I want to be able to tell the world of your Amazing Grace. I want to tell how you have shown Mercy and how you have revealed yourself to me and to us each day. I want to be the one telling that story. I want people to stop me on the street and ask how I am doing. Then I can tell them **MY** story and how God loved **ME**.

It comes in small inspirations
It brings redemption to life and work
To our lives and our work

Each day the smallest improvement is met with resounding joy. The smallest thing – the most ordinary thing brings joy and renewal of the spirit. It gives us purpose.

It comes in loving community
It comes in helping a soul find it's worth

The "Better Story" is birthed within the hearts and minds of those that we come in contact with. Our loving family – both internal and extended family brings us hope and support. It renews us each day – that love of a small community. Everyone that poked their head in Room 614 brought a smile and uplifted our spirits. An even more poignant extension of community to us was the night I opened an email and there was one that simply said, "A place to rest your head". It was from an old friend Charlie Bryant and his family. Their Aunt Mary had passed away and had left a home for them to dispose of. It was located ¾ mile from Emory – thanks to Charlie Bryant, Karen, Chuck and Seals Burdell and Celeste Porter we had a place to rest our head and Thank God for the Blessing of another day and then to be able to walk to the Hospital. The "Beauty" comes in loving community!

Redemption comes in strange places, small spaces
Calling out the best of who we are

Knowing that God loves us and cares for us and wants the best for us makes us want to live more intently. It makes us want to love each other more and more because we value each other.

And I want to add to the beauty
To tell a better story
I want to shine with the light
That's burning up inside

This is grace, an invitation to be beautiful
This is grace, an invitation

This is what God's love for us is all about. It doesn't ask anything of us other than to surrender. Grace - us receiving something that we least expect – something that is least deserved. God's unmerited love. Offered to us through the hands of others. Some we know, some we love, some we don't know but only for the Grace of God they love us. And for that I am thankful.

Redemption comes in strange places, small spaces
Calling out our best

And I want to add to the beauty
To tell a better story
I want to shine with the light
That's burning up inside

God would soon reveal to me that I can Trust Him, but I also came to understand that **He Trusts Me**! He trusts me to tell this story – He trusts me to tell a Better Story. He Trusts me to Add to the Beauty!

Dear God – just let me tell a better story!

Chapter Six

"A Smooth Stone'

Day 3 – Labor Day - Monday - Sept 6, 2010

"In the year that King Uzziah died, I saw the Lord, high and exalted, seated on a throne, and the train of his robe filled the temple" **Isaiah 6:1**

Third Day. Waiting! I had not been able to sleep at all leading up to this time. Carol was on the floor and I was in that stretch out chair thing in the room. I would alternate between sitting there staring at the room and praying and meandering outside and walking the halls of 6E. I had brought my laptop with me as well. I cope with stress by writing. As I said earlier I had been preparing all summer for a Bible Study I was to teach to a group of young men at Greensboro First United Methodist Church in Greensboro, Ga. beginning on Sept. 12, 2010. To get this into perspective here is the chronology of things as they went – Saturday, Sept. 4, 2010 Carol takes Caroline to Emory – I am at a UGA Football game in Athens – we get the initial diagnosis of Leukemia, Sunday September 5th, 2010 prep work was being done on Caroline and a bone marrow biopsy performed – initial phone calls were made to family, church etc. asking for prayers and support, Monday September 6th Dr. McLemore to give us full diagnosis and treatment protocol. Sunday, September 12th, 2010 I was scheduled to teach the Bible Study in Greensboro to our group of young men known as the Journeymen on the Max Lucado book "Facing Your Giants" – a study about the life of David centered in the Old Testament Book of the Bible --1st Samuel.

On that Monday morning, Sept. 6th I had been up early – actually had not been to sleep, maybe only fitfully for a few minutes at a time. I got my laptop and walked out into the hallway next to 614 and wrote these words, "I cannot find a smooth stone here anywhere!" As I said before I was alluding to the fact that I could find no peace at all. I was so worked up and was now waiting on the Doctors to come tell us exactly what they were going to do. My mind raced and I came to the conclusion that I could not go to Greensboro and teach that class. I told Carol and she asked me why not? I explained I had to stay with Caroline and I could not leave. Carol looked me square in the eye and said, "You have to go!" To which I asked "Why?" She gave me the most concise succinct answer I could ever have imagined. She said,"If you don't go then the Giant wins without a fight – we are fighters and you have to go!" So that was that! As I continued to contemplate what I would tell those guys at Greensboro, the thought kept recurring to me that I could not find a smooth stone at Emory anywhere. The central thought in the story of David fighting the Philistine was the line in 1 Samuel 17 verse 40 that said that David knelt down in the brook and took five smooth stones and then with his sling in his hand he "Drew near to the Philistine"! He did not draw back in fear but he moved forward toward the Giant having supreme confidence in what God would and could do with him and only one stone. He took the fight to the giant. David proved that it only took one smooth stone to do the job!

I really don't know why I wrote all of that but it came to me in a whirl at 3:15 A.M. I tried to settle back in for the day in whatever way I could. I guess at about 7:30 or 8:00 that morning the "busyness" of the day had started. Nurses, technicians, food servers, etc. were making their rounds. We were fielding calls from home and a few people dropped by that morning to say hello and pass on good wishes. I suppose at about 9 as we were waiting a dear childhood neighborhood friend came to the waiting room. It was Chip Perry. We chatted for a while and he wanted to see Chris and Caroline. They had grown up together on the cul-de-sac in Conyers. They were virtually like brothers and sisters. We had known Chip and his family since the children were infants. We went back to the room to wait on the doctor after visiting with Chip for a while in the family room on 6E. He stayed all day as we went through this most stress filled day. He waited.

The impact of the news had just about sunken in. My whole family was scared silly. Initial diagnosis on Saturday (Acute Leukemia was the broad diagnosis), Bone Marrow Biopsy on Sunday to get to the heart of the matter. From this the staff would determine exactly what strain of Leukemia she had, how to treat it, what the regimen would be, what her outlook was, how to cope! The staff had directed me to the "Pamphlet Wall" where all the literature was posted about Leukemia and blood disorders. I have to tell you that I had read just about enough of it to by this time to be scared absolutely witless. Seemed to me there was this big word called Leukemia then under that came several branches. One being Chronic Leukemia which is treated over a long period of time – it is certainly not good but it is treated in a much less radical way. The other branch is Acute Leukemia. This is very aggressive. This one means rapid onset and it means it needs a rapid response. The nurses and support staff were already treating Caroline with much intentionality with their every move. They were hustling but yet trying to keep us calm. Amy and Joy could not have been better – laughing, crying, very businesslike, very compassionate all at the same time! Time was moving very slowly for us now. Chip was still waiting in the Family room.

It had been a whirlwind – now waiting on the final diagnosis and the conference with the Doctors moved at a snail's pace. Ever so slowly it seemed like. I saw the Doctors enter the floor and begin their rounds. My heart was in my throat. I had read just enough of those books to be scared to death. I knew the words I did not want to hear!! Percentages, protocols, etc. I had already convinced myself that at this point I had done all I could do to get her situated, get her comfortable and to bring as much support as I possibly could to my daughter and to my family. I knew deep deep deep in my heart of hearts and in the core of my soul that God was firmly in control. Carol and I had prayed and given Caroline to Him. We asked that He have Mercy on our daughter and if it be His will that she would be healed. We could do no more. "God take my daughter now and do with her as you will. If you heal her we will tell your story forever and ever. If you don't heal her we will rejoice for every day we had her with us. We now understood that this was all now under your control". My prayers were going deeper; they were going deeper than they ever had before.

The Doctors were making their rounds. We were in room 614 on 6E – halfway down the second hall in the triangle configuration that makes up Emory 6E. They entered 601, then 602 then slowly coming our way. It seemed an eternity waiting on them. More fidgeting, more small talk, more prayers, more loving conversation. They turned the corner and headed down our hallway - 609, 610 ever closer. Then they were in 613 and I heard the door open and quiet whispers – then I saw them walk **PAST** our door!! My heart absolutely sank to the floor. In our human nature we tend to think the worst – you know save the worst news to last. Why had they passed us over, was it terrible news and they were saving it?? Questions, Questions! But in that moment I reassured myself that God was now absolutely in control. What I had to do was have patience and truly begin to trust – and I did.

After a long delay I finally heard the Doctors doubling back to our room after they had finished the complete rounds. I held my breath as they entered the room. It was actually the first time I sat down to listen the whole week end, but now I was prepared. I was ready for the news. I was an Offensive Lineman for the University of Georgia football team. I believe in knowing the plays. I believe in taking the attack to the enemy. I believe in being prepared. I had lived my whole life like that. Me taking charge and making things happen. Now I could not do that. I could only sit back and watch as Joy and Amy, Doctor McLemore and Dr. Ping and Dr. Hue and all the support staff as well as the other nurses now took control of the most precious thing in my life – my daughter. Now they were in control and I could only sit there and watch and sit there and pray. Always kind words – always inquisitive words. Always HOPE!

Dr. McLemore got us all situated and comfortable in the room and then he began to talk to us. He was great! **_He was actually talking to us._** Not talking to a lab rat they were about to run a test on but talking to a daughter that was scared to death. Talking to a mother and father and talking to a support group that never left her side. He said, "Well this is what we have found out." Then he began to explain that she had "T cell - Acute Lymphoblastic Leukemia". In medical slang she had A.L.L. From what I had read in the last couple of days, I actually sighed a small sigh of relief. It seemed that of the worst terrible news that we had gotten – this was the best of the terrible news. It turns out that A.L.L. is more prevalent in juvenile males. Isn't that something? Caroline would now benefit from all the research that had been done at places like St. Jude Children's Research Hospital and other Children's Hospitals with those type Leukemia patients. It was by no stretch going to be easy. In fact it was going to be a terribly hard and difficult road that she was to travel over the next period in her life, but at least now we knew what she had and Dr. McLemore explained exactly how they would approach it and how they would treat it. He gave us a pretty explicit time frame of why things happened and how they went about attacking it. We asked all our questions – some over and over again. He explained bone marrow biopsies, lumbar punctures, infusion, etc. etc over and over again preparing us for the road ahead. When Dr. McLemore was satisfied that we had exhausted our questions he and his entourage left. All things known now – plan of attack in place – now proceed with the battle. We were ready – I thought! I still did not have that smooth stone that David put in his sling. The Giant was looming ever larger and larger!

The day had now drug on and on and it was nearing 3:00 PM I suppose. We were wrung out – exhausted from stress and no sleep. We had the news and we were both concerned yet enthused at what the Doctors had said. No guarantees – each case was similar but yet way different in its individuality. We all gathered again and talked to Chip some more. He was a grown man now – very successful in his Real Estate business up at Big Canoe. He was married with a family of his own – Tina and two sons, Jackson and Alex. They were like 6 and 8 at the time. We had cried off and on all day with Chip. He loved Caroline just like a brother does. It came time for him to leave. Much as he hated to leave, he had to get home to his family at Big Canoe. That was a pretty good drive from downtown Atlanta.

Carol and I walked Chip out of the Family room and hugged him as we headed to the elevator. We were all crying our eyes out – fear and concern for Caroline but just as much for the hurt and anguish that was so evident in Chip's eyes for his friend and soul mate, Caroline. Of the kids that grew up on our block I suppose Chip and Caroline were the closest – they both possessed the same gentle spirit.

As we were approaching the elevator and saying our goodbyes Chip stopped in his tracks as the elevator door opened. While almost in a panic he stopped Carol and me. He said "Golly I almost forgot to give you something – the boys sent this to you! It came from the creek behind our house." He reached into his front pants pocket and pulled out a smooth stone. A beautiful flat smooth river rock! He pulled out from his pocket the smooth stone that I had failed to find in the brook known as Emory University Hospital; the branch of the brook that flowed through the heart of the Hospital – the Hematology Ward. On it the boys had painted a daisy, Caroline's favorite flower. They did not know it would represent the live daisy that the Doctors had told Caroline she could not have. It was beautiful! I gasped in shock. I could not get my breath when I realized what had just happened. I immediately began to weep. Carol and Chip were surprised at my reaction to the presentation of the stone. I told them you don't realize what has just happened. Then I began to recap the day and the night outside in the hallway beside room 614. **NO ONE** – I repeat **NO ONE** on Earth knew that I had written at 3:15 A.M. that morning that I had looked all over that Hospital and I could not find a smooth stone anywhere with which to fight this Giant. I was alone, I was at the end of my power, there was nothing more that I as a Dad could do to assist my daughter. The only thing I could do now was to pray to God and ask for Mercy for my daughter. I had no weapons or magic arsenal with which to fight this battle of battles. I was alone in this fight now! I had no more weapons of my own – I had to totally and sincerely Trust in God that He would be the one doing the healing. I could not go out and purchase a cure. He would be the one fighting the Giant. He would be the one giving me and my family the tools with which to fight. Now God had presented us with a tangible and physical object that was proof of His understanding and His support in this fight. With that stone gripped in Chip's hand, God had just said to me – to us – **"YOU CAN TRUST ME!"** - "I am taking the time to send you what you thought you did not have – I am sending you that smooth stone you could not find – I am even having two little boys paint a picture of a daisy on it so that Caroline can have a beautiful flower that she so desires. I will provide all that you need in this fight – your job is to Trust me now!" I fell back against the wall and worshipped! I thanked God for all He had done for my family, I thanked God for Chip – I thanked God for Chip's family in being obedient to follow through with what you prompted them to do. I thanked God for that **MOMENT!** I thanked God for that **AFFIRMATION!** I thanked God that now I knew that I could truly and wonderfully trust Him. The Creator of the Universe would take the time to send me a rock – a smooth stone – just to show me that He loved me. He was saying **"YOU CAN TRUST ME!!"**

Epilogue

"Letting Go"

These past 3 years have been at once the most trying times of our lives and at once the most fulfilling times of our lives. As a Mother and Father, Carol and I have had the privilege of watching God work in our children's lives in a way that cannot be explained. He has embedded in Caroline a strength that I **think** I knew she had but could not totally comprehend it until I saw it blossom in her soul. She portrayed grace, dignity, resolve and perseverance in a way I cannot imagine. She faced each step of the way, each day one at a time. A goal for the day – do it and check it off the list. Move on to the next item. Blood work, chemo, spinal taps, bone marrow biopsies, more chemo, more endurance. More tests. Simply amazing!

Chris rose to a level that only makes parents' hearts burst with pride and thanksgiving. His heart was broken, yet he stood by Caroline each step of the way. The whole time he was taking inventory in his heart and mind about what was really meaningful in his life. In a year's time he had seen his sister diagnosed with Leukemia, he had always been her Sir Galahad. He would swoop in when trouble loomed and save the day for her. Her Superman. Now all he could do was sit by her bed, play her music, go get her something to eat. Watch herd over all the "goings on" like a hawk. Big brother looking after his little sister just like he did on April Drive when he would hook the dog Buck up to pull her in his red wagon. Two little kids, big brother protecting his little sister. When he would walk into the room at Emory she would look at him with the same look that she always had when she was about to experience something new or frightening. He would always come to escort her with a sense of "This is my sister – treat her with respect!!" That look.

I thank God for them and the rest of our family. I can tell you that neither Carol nor I could have gone through this part of our Journey without the help of the rest of our little group.

Kelly, Sarah Grace, Amelia and Robert, they all played such a pivotal role in Caroline's recovery and our well being. They have all served to make our lives richer and deeper. I never knew that Love could be so great. I love each of them in a way that only a Father's heart can explain. I will never stop thanking God for each and every one of them – they are the greatest!!

Thank you again for coming on this Journey with us. I pray that you will find some solace and comfort in these words that we have set forth to honor and comfort you - to give you Hope and to give you Peace above all else.

There are three things that have forever been etched into my Heart and Soul. Here they are:

1- We can trust God – He wants us to Trust Him.

2- God trusts us. He trusts us enough to have us tell you this story.

3- Chip Perry was the obedient one in the whole story. He was the one that God chose to be the Courier of His assurance to me and my family. What if he had not walked down to that dry creek bed that morning with a broken heart and in his tears he was moved to reach down and take one smooth stone to bring to us in our time of desperation. Will you be a Courier for God someday?

Our Journey is not over. We have learned valuable lessons about ourselves, about each other, but most of all about God. Minutes turned into hours, hours into days, days into weeks and weeks into months. Same regimen every day, every week, every month. PICC lines, Chemo, Lumbar Punctures, visits from Doctors. Same routine - waiting day by day. Then the day we had been waiting for and the words we had been praying to hear. February 23, 2011 at Doctor Morgan McLemore's office – another Lumbar Puncture, another Bone Marrow Biopsy – then "It's Clear!!!" You are Cancer Free!!

Dr. McLemore asked Caroline "Well you want to take the PICC line out? and she goes "UHHH Yes I think so!!" We then celebrated. Caroline wanted to go eat breakfast and eat a "runny egg". It was fantastic!!

She still had to go back to Emory Clinic once a month for a small chemo and get her blood work done. **She was pronounced Cancer Free and got the all clear on February 23, 2013.** Dr. McLemore discontinued all Chemo. She has now begun the process of rejoining "regular" life with no restrictions. We are so grateful! All is fine. She is doing great!!

My calling at this point in *MY* Journey is to live by this: Acts 1:8 "You will receive power when the Holy Spirit comes upon you and you will be my witnesses in Jerusalem, Judea, Samaria and unto the ends of the Earth."

Thank you for letting me tell my story to you!

"Go in peace --- and do the little things"